Getting Things Done ...in 30 minutes

THE EXPERT GUIDE TO **DAVID ALLEN'S**

Getting Things Done

...in 30 minutes

THE 30 MINUTE EXPERT SERIES

GARAMOND PRESS

A NOTE TO THE READER: You should purchase and read the book that has been reviewed. This book is meant to accompany a reading of the reviewed book and is neither intended nor offered as a substitute for the reviewed book.

This review is unofficial and unauthorized. This book is not authorized, approved, licensed, or endorsed by David Allen or Penguin Books.

For general information on our other products and services or to obtain technical support, please contact our Customer Care Department at info@callistomedia.com.

ISBN: 978-1-62315-185-0 Print | 978-1-62315-186-7 eBook

Contents

INTRODUCTION

At a Glance

This book is an extended review of *Getting Things Done: The Art of Stress-Free Productivity,* a best-selling nonfiction book in which the author, David Allen, outlines a comprehensive system for increasing efficiency and productivity in all areas of life. Allen identifies and explains basic organizational and cognitive techniques essential to improving time-management skills, and lays out methods for uncluttering the mind and getting control over all your projects, commitments, and responsibilities.

In *Getting Things Done,* Allen encapsulates thirty years of lessons learned from his role as a corporate productivity consultant and coach to major corporations, executive clients, and institutions, consolidating his strategies into a how-to manual for those looking to accomplish more in their professional lives, personal lives, or both. Allen says genuine and exhaustive organization of one's communications, paperwork, information, and commitments leads to an expanded capacity for innovation, creativity, and self-confidence.

Since *Getting Things Done* was published in 2001, Allen has created a worldwide training and consulting company centered on the practices and methods outlined in the book—collectively described by the trademarked term *GTD*—which Allen describes as a pioneering "work-life management system."

This review begins with a concise introduction to *Getting Things Done.* This is followed by a section that provides information about the book and the author, a synopsis of reactions to the book's premises—good, bad, and in between, from professional reviewers, bloggers, and other interested readers—and a short summary of the book. Next is an in-depth discussion of the book's key concepts. Finally, the main points of this review are briefly revisited in a way that may well inspire you to get your own copy of David Allen's book and see for yourself why *Getting Things Done* is such an enduring favorite with readers, reviewers, and business writers. Also included are a list of key terms used in *Getting Things Done* and recommendations for further reading about time management and self-improvement.

Understanding *Getting Things Done*

ABOUT THE BOOK

Many people make endless to-do lists in an attempt to get organized, but often these lists lack clear direction for determining the next tangible action needed to actually complete a task. Typically, the task or project remains undone on a forgotten list.

In his career as a corporate efficiency consultant, David Allen found that specifically identifying the next concrete action necessary for each to-do item is critical to completing it. Simple techniques such as this combined into a systematic routine at home and work is what *Getting Things Done* is all about. To Allen, crossing off those finished to-do items more quickly not only increases productivity, but also relieves subconscious anxiety and helps concentrate energy in more constructive ways.

Allen sought to bring his practical knowledge of how to increase individual and institutional productivity to a wider audience by writing a detailed how-to guide describing the specific steps and procedures that lead to greater efficiency. His advice ranges from small techniques to large concepts. Allen carefully explains to readers exactly how to set up a filing system and the best way to label file folders—rudimentary organizational skills that many of us were never actually taught. But he also delves into the deeper personal benefits that he says can be derived from the consistent and habitual application of his GTD method.

Getting Things Done reached the number-one spot on both the *BusinessWeek* and the *New York Times* best-seller lists for nonfiction books on time management and self-improvement, and *Time* magazine's Jeremy Caplan described it as the "defining self-help business book" of the 2000s.

ABOUT THE AUTHOR

David Allen is the author of three books, all published by Penguin: *Getting Things Done: The Art of Stress-Free Productivity* (2001), *Ready for Anything: 52 Productivity Principles for Work and Life* (2003), and *Making It All Work: Winning at the Game of Work and Business of Life* (2008). He is founder and chairman of the David Allen Company, which he started with his wife, Kathryn, in 1996. It is now an international consulting and training company, and Allen and his colleagues present lectures and seminars on his trademarked Getting Things Done "work-life management system," widely known as GTD. The GTD method is the foundation of Allen's consulting and coaching work for corporations and organizations such as Microsoft and the World Bank. Allen says his method is distilled from lessons learned over the past thirty years in the corporate training world.

Originally from Shreveport, Louisiana, Allen received a BA from New College of Florida. According to a 2007 *Wired* magazine profile, Allen moved to California in 1968 for graduate study at the University of California at Berkeley, but eventually dropped out and went through a troubled period that included heroin use and involuntary commitment at Napa State Hospital.

Bouncing back from adversity, Allen became deeply involved in the human potential and personal growth movements, and by the early 1980s he was a facilitator of a self-help program called Insight. Around the same time, a manager at aerospace company Lockheed recruited him as a consultant, and Allen developed a seminar that combined New Age ideas with corporate human resources training methods. This led to a career as an executive coach, management consultant, and trainer focused on increasing personal and companywide productivity and efficiency.

CRITICAL RECEPTION

The Upside

Acclaim for *Getting Things Done* has been widespread and passionate since its initial publication in 2001, and positive reviews of the book and interviews with David Allen about the GTD method have appeared in the *New York Times*, the *Atlantic* magazine, the *Wall Street Journal*, and the *San Francisco Chronicle*; business and technology magazines such as *Fast Company*, *Success*, *Entrepreneur*, and *Wired*; and academic journals such as the *Chronicle of Higher Education* and *Long Range Planning: International Journal of Strategic Management*.

Today the GTD method is the focus of online fans—such as *43Folders* (a blog whose URL is a reference to the forty-three file folders Allen recommends using to set up a filing system), Lifehacker.com, and GTD.Marvelz.com.

San Francisco Chronicle columnist James Temple interviewed Allen in 2012 and said GTD is "a self-help system to be sure, but one that's earned real credibility in corporate America, with Coca-Cola, Microsoft, McDonald's and Walmart among the many clients."

Writing in the British newspaper the *Guardian* in 2005, Ben Hammersley wrote, "For me, as with the hundreds of thousands around the world who press the book into their friends' hands with fire in their eyes, Allen's ideas are nothing short of life-changing."

Fast Company editor Keith H. Hammonds wrote in 2000, "David Allen [is] one of the world's most influential thinkers on personal productivity."

In an article written for *Business 2.0* and published in *CNN Money*, Paul Keegan said, "The effect of Allen's teachings on harried office workers can seem miraculous," and writing for *Fortune Small Business*, Chris Taylor said:

> In the past four years I have encountered just one great system for organizing my entire life. It's the same one that has swept Silicon Valley, rules the roost at Google and recently inspired some of the most innovative personal-management software I've yet seen. Converts refer to it by just three letters: GTD.

The Downside

Positive reviews of *Getting Things Done* have greatly outweighed negative ones in print and the blogosphere over the past decade. Those who do criticize the book primarily say it offers recycled ideas and concepts.

IT expert Luc Glasbeek, writing on his blog, *Workplace Prosperity*, points out that in 1976—twenty-five years before Allen's book was published—a "productivity expert" named Edwin C. Bliss published a book titled *Getting Things Done*. "A time-management expert explains how to set priorities according to personal goals, delegate authority and responsibility, decrease stress and increase energy, and create a user-friendly environment," reads the description of Bliss's book on Amazon.com, a summary that could describe Allen's book as well. Allen has not addressed the remarkable similarities between his now-trademarked ideas and Bliss's antecedent work with the same title and key themes, but other bloggers such as Douglas Johnston and Erin Doland have taken note of the parallels.

Writing for the American Library Association, Mary Whaley calls the book, "an infomercial for the author's consulting practice," while reader reviews on Amazon.com opine that "this book reads more like a sales pitch than a guide to getting organized. Online resources actually explain Allen's concept far better than he does, because he's too busy trying to be cute and clever to express his ideas succinctly."

Another reader wrote, "*Getting Things Done* is terribly painful to read. The problem stems mainly from the fact that there are about fifty pages in the book that contain real information. The other two hundred pages are—no joke—almost word-for-word rehash of those fifty pages." And another reader commented, "This whole book really could have been summarized in ten pages. The rest is just fluff, mindless personal commentary on how to organize stuff without any reason on why Allen's way is better than other ways he criticizes in the opening."

Zenhabits blogger Leo Babauta writes that David Allen's GTD method "is based on productivity advice that has been around for generations—each productivity guru improving on the previous one a little, but basically giving the same advice. GTD isn't revolutionary—it's a great system compiled from advice that's been around for awhile."

SYNOPSIS

To David Allen, the mushrooming of technology in the industrialized world over the past few decades has not simplified our work or personal lives. On the contrary, each new day ushers in a stream of incoming e-mail and Facebook messages; cell phones connect us anywhere, anytime; and most people now have jobs involving "knowledge work," as business management icon Peter Drucker calls it, for which there are no clear-cut parameters and criteria for completion.

A century ago, the vast majority of Americans worked at manual labor, and it was obvious when a job was finished: the butter was churned, the woodpile chopped and stacked, and the crops sown. These days we spend a lot less time performing physical chores, but there is scant division between work and personal life, and for many, their myriad work projects could always be better, more comprehensive, more effective. Increased leisure time has equated to an overwhelming number of choices about what to do with that free time, and a barrage of options, loose ends, and unfulfilled ambitions nag at the back of our minds as a result.

To Allen, this ambiguity generates more stress and anxiety than we realize, and it prevents us from reaching our full productive and energetic capacities. Much of our anxiety, he says, comes from a peculiarity of the human mind: we can't possibly remember all the commitments we have made and things we must do at home and at work. Hence the popularity of date books and planners. Nevertheless, our subconsciousness doggedly registers all the looming deadlines and tasks still to be done and causes the mind to brood at a deep level. An indefinite but potent awareness of these open loops, as Allen calls them, is the source of our modern angst.

It is therefore essential to get organized in a thorough and habitual way to combat this open-ended mental tension. The simple act of writing down all the to-do tasks floating in your short-term memory will free up mental space for more creative, big-picture thinking. Gathering together all the paperwork in your environment and putting it in one place for processing is another way to start increasing your productivity.

A chief goal of the GTD method is to achieve a "mind like water," a martial arts term that describes a state of ideal preparedness and calm, like a still pond. When a stone is tossed in, the surface will react in a way that is "totally appropriate to the force and mass of the input; then it returns to calm. It doesn't overreact or underreact," explains Allen.

In *Getting Things Done*, Allen describes in detail how to set up a comprehensive system for dealing with all the mental and physical "stuff," as he calls it, that clutters our mind, living spaces, and workplaces; stifles energy; and interferes with a clear mind. He describes five discrete stages of managing professional and personal workflow in a relaxed and controlled manner. When completed in an ordered and habitual fashion, these five stages will seamlessly take care of business on all fronts.

First, says Allen, is collection. That means getting everything out of your head and written down. Writing down errands, tasks, ideas, and goals on dedicated to-do lists is effective, as long as the next stage is faithfully executed; that's processing, which is identifying the next concrete action needed to complete the task, advance the project, or realize the idea. This next-action thinking is crucial to sustaining focus on the task at hand.

Allen's third stage is organizing—following certain tips and techniques for processing and organizing workflow, such as grouping together tasks by subject or context. The fourth stage is reviewing all your options and establishing a fixed procedure for regular review. Routinely reviewing your various to-do lists and action items on a regular basis will ensure follow-through and completion.

Finally, after all that collecting, sifting, and reviewing, the last stage is to take action.

Key Concepts of *Getting Things Done*

According to David Allen, stress-free productivity starts with **collection**, a process of gathering together all your stuff—every physical and mental item that clutters your environment or mind—and putting it in one big in-basket. Then comes using **next-action thinking and the two-minute rule** to decide how to handle each in-basket item. Finally, Allen explains why a **weekly review** will make the GTD method most effective.

I. COLLECTION

Collection is the starting point for the GTD organizing system. Allen defines collection as the act of gathering the physical paperwork that surrounds you in the form of stacks of reports on the floor next to your desk, or receipts stuffed in your glove box or wallet, plus all your calendar notes and reminders, into one specific place he calls the in-basket.

It also means writing down—ideally, on separate pieces of paper, so that each paper is a tangible placeholder in your in-basket—all abstract projects, ideas, errands, grocery lists . . . whatever is on your mind that you need to take care of, realize, or complete. All—and the emphasis is on *all*—unfinished tasks, errands, projects, and paperwork that don't forever belong in their current place are initially gathered together (or written down) as an "inventory of open loops." Open loops are all the mental flotsam and jetsam in our lives that float around in our subconsciousness: all the things that need to be done, handled, or considered. It usually takes anywhere from one hour to six hours just to get all these loose ends together in one spot.

"In order for your mind to let go of the lower-level task of trying to hang on to everything, you have to know that you have truly captured *everything* that might represent something you have to do, and that at some point in the near future you will process and review all of it," Allen says. Been meaning to clean out your toolshed? Write "clean toolshed" on a piece of paper and put it in the in-basket. Need to buy new running shoes? Write down "buy running shoes" on another piece of paper and drop it in the in-basket. Later, during the processing stage, you will include this item on your to-do list for things you need from a particular store.

Allen calls this organizing by context. Instead of writing down one long to-do list, you organize your action items into several different to-do lists by context—one list for items to buy at the grocery store, another list for things to buy at the hardware store, another list for phone calls to make, and so on. That way, when you are walking through the doors of the grocery or hardware store, you have a list in hand that you know contains all the items you need to buy.

To accommodate the collection process, Allen recommends establishing a "central cockpit of control," typically a home office, workplace office, or desk space. Several pages of *Getting Things Done* are dedicated to the specific organizational tools necessary to begin the collection process, including file folders, the importance of getting your own labeler, and basic office supplies such as a stapler, wastebasket, and paper trays.

A vital organization tool is your own personal filing system, preferably alphabetical, in which you can easily file all the in-basket items that require no action but are, for example, important documents or necessary receipts that you must keep. These will immediately go into your storage files as you work your way through your in-basket during the initial processing period.

Collection is essentially cleaning house—methodically accumulating each and every scrap of paper, receipt, business card, printed-out e-mail, and so on, as well as written notes about abstract tasks and projects, into one place for processing. Allen recommends starting with your desktop, then moving to the drawers, cabinets, bookshelves, and so on, until your entire physical environment is cleared of loose paperwork and items.

Allen compares collecting all the abstract mental "stuff" that you are worried about, planning, responsible for, need to buy while running errands, and so forth to emptying your short-term memory, just as you would erase your computer's RAM (random-access memory) to create more space. Allen says the brain's short-term memory has only so much storage space, and if you're filling it up with the minutiae of daily life, you don't have capacity for more expansive, creative, and productive thoughts. He recommends conducting a mind-sweep during the collection process to get every nagging item out of your head, onto a piece of paper, and into your in-basket so that you can start taking action.

Not only will the collection phase of the GTD method organize your physical environment and clear your mind, but "when people with whom you interact notice that without fail you receive, process, and organize in an airtight manner the exchanges and agreements they have with you, they begin to trust you in a unique way," writes Allen. Becoming habitually ultra-organized is key to improving your reputation as someone who is productive and energetic, and collection is the place to start.

Allen stresses that it is important to dedicate a block of time solely to the task of collection, and to not get distracted by taking action on some items in a random fashion. The point is to collect *everything* together in a methodical way *before* starting the processing phase.

Examples from Getting Things Done

- Allen suggests putting together a trigger list, which is an item-by-item list of things that jog your memory about something that needs to be done or completed, and therefore collected and put in the in-basket. His own list includes items such as commitments or promises to others, legal issues, promotion, supplies, professional development, professional wardrobe, home and household, errands, and community and civic issues. If you develop a trigger list template that includes every aspect of your life, then every week you can review it to make sure there is nothing lurking in your subconsciousness that will drain your mental energy and cause anxiety. When your trigger list causes you to remember a to-do item, it goes into your in-basket.

- Once you're past the initial all-inclusive collection phase, you're not done with collection. You should make routine collection a habit. Allen says when he returns from a long business trip, he gathers all the business cards, reports, and meeting notes he picked up along the way and places them in his in-basket for processing.
- If a physical item is too big to place in the collection in-basket, Allen jots down a sentence about the item on a plain piece of paper. For example, if you've been meaning to change the artwork on your office wall, write "artwork on office wall" and the date and put it in the in-basket along with all the other collection items for processing. Or if you have an attic full of junk you've intended to clear out for years, write down "clean attic" on a piece of paper, and into the in-basket it goes. Any and all abstract projects get processed out of the in-basket in the same way as those stacks of unread magazines, unanswered e-mails, and legal pads full of notes.
- "As soon as you attach a 'should,' 'need to,' or 'ought to' to an item, it becomes an incomplete," writes Allen. It then needs to go into the in-basket "until you have a few moments to decide what they are and what, if anything, you're going to do about them."
- What if the in-basket gets too full during the all-important collection stage? Make piles around it. The crucial aspect of the process is that you will be going through each and every in-basket item, from top to bottom in order, and handling everything sequentially. You will eventually get to the page that reads "artwork on office wall" or "clean attic," and take appropriate action at that time.

Applying the Concept

- **Clean out the junk drawer.** For decades, the ubiquitous junk drawer has been the subject of jokes in every household. But to Allen, that catchall drawer is no laughing matter; it's a festering black hole that's preying on your subconscious mind and blunting your productivity. Followers of the GTD method would vanquish that drawer by dumping the entire contents into the in-basket, and then processing each item one by one, finding a permanent and proper home for every item.

- **Sort all your mail.** Your e-mail account is already collecting items for you, automatically sorting incoming messages and placing them in the cyber version of the in-basket. Your voice mail does the same for phone messages, and even the neighborhood letter carrier is helping you out by collecting mail addressed to you and delivering it to your home or office. But all these inputs require attention and action, so they will need to go, in some form, into the physical in-basket you've created for the GTD method.

- **Clean out your mental clutter.** Don't hesitate to write down the grandiose and outrageous ideas that live at the back of your mind, such as saving the environment, raising the socioeconomic status of women in the third world, or finding a cure for cancer. Getting these ideas out of your mind, onto a concrete piece of paper, and into the in-basket—alongside the placeholders for remembering to buy dog food and request a new ATM card—can help focus your attention on figuring out your true long-term goals. The end result of the collection phase should be a total power washing of your mind. This is what Allen calls a mind-sweep—cleaning out all the old ideas and making room for more creative and focused thinking.

II. NEXT-ACTION THINKING AND THE TWO-MINUTE RULE

Next-action thinking is *the* central aspect of David Allen's organizational method. It involves identifying the next specific, concrete action needed to complete a particular task, errand, project, or goal. Some actions will be simple, such as making a phone call or signing off on a purchasing request. Other, more complex tasks are easy to put off because many people don't identify what actions are really needed to complete them, says Allen. Lengthy to-do lists languish undone because of this vagueness. Success with Allen's GTD method results from making a firm decision about what to do next with each in-basket item after collection.

That doesn't mean you have to act immediately on all the hundreds of items that ended up in your in-basket after the collection phase. It simply means grouping that task together with similar ones (grouping by context) and identifying the next action to be taken. This way, when you have the time, you can complete the next action on that subgroup as a whole—and thus get more done with less effort.

In *Getting Things Done,* Allen includes a flowchart that illustrates the decision-making process for each in-basket item. First is to determine the exact nature of the item and whether it is actionable. If not, it goes either in the trash, in a tickler file for future action, or in your permanent storage files. If there is a distinct, identifiable action to take on the item, determine what that action is, then figure out whether to "do it, delegate it, or defer it," as Allen summarizes.

This is when the two-minute rule comes into play. If the task can be done in less than two minutes, do it immediately, on the spot. Make that call, book that appointment online, compose and send that e-mail. If the action will take more than two minutes, the next step is to either delegate the task to someone who can take care of it more effectively, or move it to a place in your established filing system to work on later. This filing system becomes a sort of "pending" file—the physical backup of your to-do list.

"All you really need is lists and folders," Allen writes, to make the GTD method work. He suggests seven basic types of "pending" folders that will hold any tasks or in-basket items that take longer than two minutes to accomplish:

- Someday/maybe
- Next actions
- Projects
- Project support materials
- Waiting for
- Actions or information that go on your calendar
- Reference material you want to keep on hand

That piece of paper on which you wrote "raising the socioeconomic status of women in the third world" would go into the "someday/maybe" folder for periodic review. If you haven't determined the next concrete action—such as "donate one hundred dollars to international microlending nongovernmental organization via their website"—there is still value in placing it in the "someday/maybe" folder and reviewing it every so often, because it gets that particular open loop off your mind.

For every actionable item in your collected in-basket, run through the "do it, delegate it, or defer it" set of options, says Allen. If it gets deferred to one of the pending folders, make sure you group it together with similar context items. For example, all the phone calls you need to make go on one list, so that when you have a ten-minute wait for the next train, you can start making calls and crossing them off.

Allen suggests creating contextual to-do lists such as "errands," "calls," and "waiting for." After deciding what the next action will be, each in-basket item can go on the appropriate list, and everything is grouped for completion. Allen's own "waiting for" file is the place he puts items that depend on someone else taking action before he can complete it. Each person can come up with his or her own file names for subgroups, as long as the next actions are identified.

Grouping to-do items together by context on accessible lists will ensure that during lull periods in your workday, you always have a handy prompt for actionable items. Or when you are out running errands, you can pull up your "errands" list on your smartphone and start crossing items off as you complete them, and you won't forget anything.

Allen urges readers to avoid cherry-picking when processing your inbox, that is, using next-action thinking on the easy or obvious tasks but leaving the more complex ones for later. He calls this emergency scanning. Instead, says Allen, always work from top to bottom, processing each and every item in sequence, one at a time, without making a judgment about the item's priority. This will ensure that everything gets dealt with and psychic anxiety about pending items is relieved.

During the processing phase, never put anything back into the in-basket. This isn't always easy, because many in-basket items are ambiguous or so complex that it's hard to know where to start. But it's critical that every item be processed in order and the next action decided for each of your in-basket items.

"You'll be surprised how many two-minute actions you can perform on even your most critical projects," writes Allen, and he reminds readers of what Mark Twain said on the subject: "The secret of getting ahead is getting started." Allen adds, "The secret of getting started is breaking your complex, overwhelming tasks into smaller management tasks and then starting on the first one."

This is precisely what next-action thinking is—figuring out the next concrete action needed on each item and then doing that action immediately if it will take less than two minutes. If it will take longer, put it in one of the seven folders that you will be taking action on as soon as possible.

Examples from Getting Things Done

- Allen offers the following example of why it's important to group tasks by context. If you have a flashlight stuck in a drawer with dead batteries, you tend to remember that you need fresh batteries only when you try to use the flashlight. That does you no good. The time you need to remember the batteries is when you pass a store that sells them. If the flashlight battery issue was in your in-basket and ended up grouped on the "hardware store" list, the next time you went to the store you'd remember to get those batteries.

- Allen offers a sample to-do list on which the first three items are "clean the garage," "do my taxes," and "conference I'm going to." What is the next action to take on all three? For the first one, cleaning the garage, it may seem to be a case of simply getting in there and doing it. What is preventing that from happening? Allen points out that when he thinks about it, he realizes there is a large refrigerator in the garage that he wants to remove and perhaps donate to his friend's camp. It's really dealing with the refrigerator that's holding up completion of "clean the garage." In that case, the next action would be for him to call his friend to see if he wants the old refrigerator; if not, find somewhere else to donate it. As for the taxes, again, Allen examines this to-do item to determine the next action, which is getting back a certain financial report from his trust company before he can complete his taxes. So this in-basket item would go into the "waiting for" file for future action. Finally, "conference I'm going to" is not an actionable to-do item. It is just a reminder that he needs to prepare for it. When he thinks about this to-do item, he realizes he needs to e-mail a coworker to see if she is going to assemble a press kit for the conference, so the next-action item would be "e-mail Sandra with questions about press kit." In this case, sending the e-mail would take less than two minutes, so he does this on the spot while he's processing this particular to-do list.

- Allen says he learned of the power of next-action thinking from a fellow management consultant who began picking up each piece of paper on an executive's desk and "forcing him to decide what the very next thing was that he had to do to move it forward." Allen says he has noticed an "extraordinary shift in energy and productivity" when people start using next-action thinking consistently and routinely. He believes identifying the next concrete, specific action needed to further projects or complete tasks is of the utmost importance in transforming your organizational skills and boosting productivity. Furthermore, according to Allen, next-action thinking is valuable for bringing accountability, clarity, empowerment, and productivity to tasks: accountability because it pinpoints who is responsible for a certain action; clarity because it simplifies what is needed to be done; empowerment because it will bring a sense of control to your workflow; and productivity because it ensures that concrete plans are made to move forward with any task or long-term project.

Applying the Concept

- **Get in the habit of next-action thinking by breaking down each to-do item into a series of steps.** If you want to brighten up your bedroom with a new coat of robin egg blue paint, don't write "paint bedroom" on your list. Rather, write down the project as a series of steps. Maybe the first would be "check garage for paint tools." Next, on your "errands" list you'd put a subhead of "hardware store." There you would write, "buy gallon of paint, paintbrushes, roller, paint tray, drop cloth, and painter's tape."
- **When processing your inbox items, the two-minute rule can be flexible.** If you have a large block of time to focus on processing, you can extend the time limit to five minutes to get more done on a particu-

lar task. If you are in a hurry but want to stay on top of your in-basket, you can decrease it to a minute to help you crank through the pile.

- **Break things down into small, manageable steps.** Procrastination is really the manifestation of fear and lack of control, and next-action thinking can mitigate that by providing a concrete step the mind can recognize as progress. Decide the next action as soon as a task or project comes on your radar, and before your imagination can blow it up into something fearsome and overwhelming. If you've volunteered to organize a surprise birthday party with one hundred guests, instead of writing "surprise party" on a to-do list, spend two minutes figuring out the necessary next steps and then write down small, distinct actions. On your "calls" list, you would write specific items like "call park district to reserve Pinecone picnic area for June 5," and "call Bonnie's Catering and order one hundred box lunches for pickup on morning of June 5."

III. WEEKLY REVIEW

Now you've gotten in the habit of collecting everything into your in-basket, processing each item by deciding the next action needed, and organizing those actions by context. Getting everything in your mental storage down on a piece of paper or laptop notepad and onto the appropriate to-do lists helps you gain control of all your tasks. But to get things done, you need to actively and regularly review your lists and continually assess what can move to the front burner and what can be relegated to the pending files. It's sort of like an ongoing chess game where you are rearranging the pieces to maintain the most effective strategy.

A weekly review of all your action folders will make sure you stay on top of the workflow. The weekly review verifies that you've got all your tasks and projects on the correct lists and are taking real action to move each item forward or complete it.

Allen recommends spending at least an hour each week going over your next-action lists and pending files and again applying the two-minute rule to handle all the tasks that can be done at that time. It's also the time, as Allen says, to "gather and process all your 'stuff,' review your system, update your lists, and get clean, clear, current, and complete."

When discussing the weekly review, Allen explains his six-level model for reviewing, which uses aviation terminology to illustrate different degrees of evaluation. The highest level is fifty thousand feet. At this most far-reaching and encompassing level, you look at your overall life goals. At forty thousand feet, you're looking at your three- to five-year goals and envisioning what you want to happen and create during that period. Dropping down, thirty thousand feet is the level at which you examine your one- to two-year goals and objectives. At twenty thousand feet you're assessing your present areas of responsibility in work and your personal life, and at ten thousand feet you're reviewing your current long- and short-term projects. Finally, at runway level, you're reviewing your current actionable item lists that include the phone calls you need to make, the errands you need to run, and so forth.

Looking at your entire workflow in these terms will help you set priorities and achieve a healthful balance in managing all levels of your life. Allen advises working from the bottom up when using this model; making sure the runway and ten-thousand-foot levels are organized and operational will free up more psychic RAM for you to focus on fifty-thousand-foot-level thinking and dreaming.

Another key aspect of the weekly review is that it ensures your organizational system will stay current and effective over time. It's crucial that you build a system in which you can place your wholehearted trust. Consistently and faithfully doing a weekly review of all your actionable lists and files provides a sense of trust that the system is working to your advantage as tasks are completed and projects furthered.

For many practitioners of GTD, the weekly review consists of assessing four main areas: calendar, to-do lists, projects folders, and e-mail. Maintaining a large, easy-to-read online or physical calendar as one of your key organizational tools will help you track appointments, meetings, and deadlines as you process time-sensitive items in your in-basket.

During the weekly review, also look at your "someday/maybe" and long-term projects lists to see if progress can be made on either. Some people force themselves to choose dated items on the "someday/maybe" list and turn them into actionable projects, complete with next steps, to get the ball rolling and prevent the projects from languishing forever on the "someday" list.

As recommended during the initial collection phase, it helps to create a trigger list template enumerating every conceivable area of your daily life that needs attention. Keep that template handy during the weekly review as well, so you can refer to it and confirm that you've captured everything on your mind and put it into the in-basket. To Allen, the weekly review is also a chance to get a bird's-eye view of your whole system, to see the big picture, so you are intimately familiar with everything that's on your plate at all times.

As you move forward with the GTD method, Allen suggests you learn to say no to more requests. These days many people take on way more than they can ever hope to handle, and then they feel guilty for not accomplishing it all. Increasing productivity and easing psychic drag depends on your getting a complete handle on your responsibilities and making the tough decisions about what to take on and what to refuse or toss out.

Examples from Getting Things Done

- Allen points out that many individuals feel the least anxiety at work in the days leading up to a planned vacation. This is not due to the vacation itself, but because they have wrapped up all their loose ends and "cleaned up, closed up, clarified, and renegotiated" their responsibilities. Most people clear their in-basket, delegate tasks to others in their absence, and conduct a mind-sweep to capture and close all the open loops before they head to the airport. Allen suggests that this process should be completed weekly rather than annually, to keep the mind focused on concrete and actionable lists. An ideal time to do this weekly review is on a Friday afternoon or Monday morning.

- To assist in the weekly review, Allen recommends setting up a tickler file—a calendar in three-dimensional form. This tickler, or reminder, filing system comprises forty-three file folders, thirty-one of which are labeled one through thirty-one for the days of the month, and twelve of which are labeled with each month of the year. In a file drawer or desktop rack, the files labeled by days of the month are in front and the remaining monthly folders are in the rear. In the processing phase of the GTD method, the tickler file will be the place you drop paper-based reminders in date-specific folders. At the start of each day, check that date's folder to get tangible prompts of things you need to take care of on that particular day, such as appointments, business meetings, or forms that need to be filled out and mailed.
- Allen cautions that the tickler file system works well only if you review it each and every day, and move the previous day's folder to the back and the current day's folder to the front. If you go away, diligently go through the files for the days you will be gone, and take action on the contents before your departure.

Applying the Concept

- **Keep your e-mail inbox as empty as possible at all times.** This doesn't mean you answer every request or do every task contained in incoming e-mails, just that you rigorously delete all unnecessary e-mails, complete the items or tasks that will take two minutes or less, and then organize the remaining ones into your pending or action folders. Make sure you review these folders often so nothing falls through the cracks.

- **Use your cell phone as an organizational tool.** If you've had a dinner meeting with a client and got a great idea for that client's account on your way home in the cab, jot it down in the "notes" section of your smartphone. The weekly review is a good time to empty all those notes, numbers, and important texts from your cell phone—an important organizational tool that is often overlooked during the collection phase. If you use a physical calendar on your desk to keep track of things, be sure to sync that info on your smartphone so the two work in tandem to keep you on top of things.
- **Enjoy your newfound productivity.** Once you've got your new system up and running, one of the most pleasurable aspects of the weekly review will be checking off completed items and moving them off all your lists. It's a time to review all the undone tasks and projects, yes, but it's also a time to purge paperwork you no longer need, delete e-mails and voice mails, and move an actionable project folder into your permanent "done" files. The more productive you become, the more stuff you'll be accomplishing, crossing off your lists, and dumping in the trash. This clearing of files is just as important as figuring out the next action to take on things undone.

Key Takeaways

- The two key ingredients for controlling your workflow and being relaxed while doing it are (1) having clearly defined projects and the next actions required to move them to completion, and (2) setting up reminders in a trusted system that you regularly review.
- Start by cataloging, in a methodical and routine manner, every single part of your work and personal life that demands your attention and action. This means collecting all the physical and paper-based items in your envi-

ronment and putting them in one place for processing, referred to simply as your in-basket. Likewise, increasing productivity and reducing angst depends on getting all the to-do items, errands, and ideas out of your head and onto a piece of paper or electronic notepad so that you can focus your mental energy on actually getting things done.

- Once you've gathered together every single item or task, physical and mental, that you need to take care of, it's critical to spend a few moments on each task deciding what is the specific next action to take to complete it. If that action will take less than two minutes, do it immediately. If it will take longer, catalog the task or project in one of a handful of organizing to-do lists that you group together by context. Processing each and every in-basket item in a systematic and sequential manner will ensure that everything gets listed and organized, and concrete steps are taken toward completion.
- When you have your organizing system up and running, a critical aspect to its success is conducting a routine weekly review to purge completed items, moving projects around among your handful of action folders—based on priority and context—and making sure your day-to-day activities are in line with your long-term goals.
- The key to the method's success is doing all five stages of the GTD method at once: collect, process, organize, review, and do. *Collect* means getting everything written down on dedicated to-do lists. *Process* means identifying the concrete action needed to complete each. Next, organize your workflow. *Review* means reviewing your options for what to do about each task; routinely reviewing your various to-do lists and action items will ensure follow-through and completion. And finally, take action.

CONCLUSION

A Final Word

In the years since David Allen published *Getting Things Done*, his method and efficiency ideas have attracted thousands of followers who use them in both their professional and personal lives to get organized in a meaningful way. There are dozens of GTD "groupie" websites where those dedicated to Allen's system discuss his latest ideas and give each other pointers on how to better use the GTD method, and the David Allen Company annually earns millions selling supplementary GTD resources, consulting services, and presentations to individuals and companies around the world.

At the heart of this method to master workflow is a commonsense set of organizational steps that together create a routine and consistent way of dealing with one's total environment. First and foremost is Allen's recommendation to purge your mind of every single nagging thought—from the need to buy butter and milk to a vague plan to return to school to get your master's degree—by writing it down. Conducting a mind-sweep to clear out the clutter in your short-term memory will open up mental space to focus on larger questions. Once all the tasks and to-do items that you need to take care of daily are not cluttering up your mind and causing confusion and anxiety, you can tackle everything more productively because you are relaxed and feel in control.

Collecting everything you need to take care of and making concrete decisions about the very next action to take on each task are the two key objectives of Allen's system. Rather than compose lists of ill-defined projects or tasks, it's crucial to instead identify next actions and then organize these actions by context. Contextualizing your tasks, big and small, will make them easier to accomplish and make you a more productive and energetic person.

Key Terms

collection the first of Allen's five stages of mastering workflow, collection is the physical act of gathering in one place all the paper-based, electronic, and abstract things that need your attention and **processing**. It can be stacks of reports that need perusing or receipts stuffed in a jacket pocket, as well as ideas or concepts in the mind that require action to take care of, realize, or complete.

context organizing to-do items by context means grouping them together by the actual location at which they need to be processed. For example, composing an e-mail, looking up a restaurant menu on a website, and writing a report all need to be done at a computer, so these to-do items would be grouped on an "at computer" list. Then the next time you are sitting in front of your laptop, you can open that list and start accomplishing things. Similarly, things like "buy a new mouse" and "get file folders" would go on the "errands" list under "office supply store."

decision-making criteria Allen outlines four distinct criteria for deciding how to take action during the **processing** phase of the GTD method. Choosing how to handle each item in your **in-basket** involves determining the **context** of the item, how much energy and time you have at the moment to spend on the item, and its priority.

doing the fifth stage of workflow management, doing means taking the necessary next action that will further the item or task toward completion.

emergency scanning picking through your one big **in-basket** and choosing to act on only the most pressing matters or tasks—or only on the items you feel like dealing with. Allen advises against falling into this unproductive trap. Instead, he recommends processing each and every item in order, without judgment as to its priority.

in-basket the place where you put all the physical items in your life that need to be processed or acted on in some way, along with any note-taking device, paper or electronic, that will work for you. Allen says, "You should have as many in-baskets as you need and as few as you can get by with."

knowledge work a term coined by management expert Peter Drucker and referenced heavily by Allen, knowledge work is work that is ill-defined and lacks clear boundaries, unlike the manual or factory labor of days gone by. In jobs entailing knowledge work, it's hard to know when something is wholly completed or in its most optimal state.

mind-sweep cleaning out your short-term memory by mentally searching for all possible to-do tasks, abstract goals, ideas, and problems. Writing them down can help with the mind-sweep by reminding you of all the concepts that are floating around in your head at any given moment; after you write them down, you can start taking action.

next-action decisions a crucial aspect of Allen's method, next-action decision making means identifying the next tangible action needed to complete a particular task, errand, project, or goal. This second phase of the GTD method is concretely choosing the next action needed for each **in-basket** item and grouping that task with similar ones so that when you have the time, you can complete the next actions in that group.

open loops the mental commitments, flotsam, and jetsam in your mind that pull at your attention but don't belong where they are, the way they are. This can be as big-picture as "cure cancer" or as small as "buy cat litter."

processing this second phase of the GTD method involves deciding what next action is needed on each **in-basket** item and organizing them by **context** into the appropriate pending file or action folder. If an **in-basket** task or project can be completed within two minutes, it is processed on the spot. If it takes longer, processing the item means placing it on one of your action lists for future handling.

stuff Allen defines this as "anything you have allowed into your psychological or physical world that doesn't belong where it is, but for which you haven't yet determined the desired outcome and the next action step."

trigger list an item-by-item list of things that jog your memory about something that needs to be done or completed, and therefore is collected and put in the **in-basket**. These triggers might be promises or commitments, professional development goals, or legal issues. When your trigger list causes you to remember a to-do item, it goes into your **in-basket**.

two-minute rule Allen's standard for how long it should take to **process** items in your **in-basket**, and "more or less the point where it starts taking longer to store and track an item than to deal with it the first time it's in your hands." As you go through your **in-basket** and identify the **context** of each item, quickly think about the approximate time it will take to complete. Allen uses an egg timer to gauge this, and if it's within the two-minute rule, he performs the task immediately without filing it under a further to-do list.

Recommended Reading

In addition to David Allen's ***Getting Things Done: The Art of Stress-Free Productivity*** (Penguin, 2001), the following books are recommended for anyone who wants to learn better time-management skills, increase workplace and personal productivity, and get more organized.

David Allen, *Making It All Work: Winning at the Game of Work and the Business of Life* (Penguin, 2008)

Allen's second follow-up to his best-selling *Getting Things Done, Making It All Work* further expounds on the GTD method and explains that if his first book provides a toolkit to better productivity, this sequel offers a road map to getting organized and creating the life you want to lead.

Dale Carnegie, *How to Win Friends and Influence People*, reissue edition (Simon & Schuster, 2009)

More than seventy years after its publication in 1936, this timeless classic remains in print. Recent editions have been updated with contemporary examples. It's a popular book with those looking to improve their interactions with others and become more effective in everyday life, as well as be more persuasive.

Robert B. Cialdini, *Influence: The Psychology of Persuasion*, revised edition (William Morrow, 2006)

First published in the early 1980s, *Influence* has become a standard textbook used in business, psychology, and sociology classrooms around the country. Cialdini delves deep into sociological research to unearth the science behind persuasion and the keys to the consumer mind when it comes to sales and purchasing. Cialdini teaches his readers seven basic principles behind influence, how they work to get us to say yes, and how we can guard against them.

Stephen R. Covey, *The 7 Habits of Highly Effective People: Powerful Lessons in Personal Change*, revised edition (Simon & Schuster, 2004)

This book, exploring Covey's "principle-centered philosophy," has sold millions of copies. It examines personal efficiency and offers practical guidelines to help people set goals and improve their lives and relationships.

Peter F. Drucker, *The Effective Executive: The Definitive Guide to Getting the Right Things Done*, revised edition (HarperBusiness, 2006)

Considered the father of the management consulting industry, Drucker had a huge impact on the modern corporation and management thinking. This book zeros in on improving time-management skills, increasing productivity, and choosing one's battles and successes. While geared toward business executives, anyone can apply the principles in this book to his or her own life.

Napoleon Hill, *Think and Grow Rich*, reissue edition (Tribeca, 2013)

This self-improvement book is more focused on the material aspects of life and how to improve one's personal fortune. It also examines the effect positive thinking can have on anyone's life and offers tips and principles that lead to personal achievement. First published during the Great Depression, it remains in print and a best seller.

Jeffrey Pfeffer, *Power: Why Some People Have It and Others Don't* (HarperBusiness, 2010)

Pfeffer, a Stanford University professor, examines the nature of power and performance and explores why CEOs, presidents, and world leaders get to those positions. Pfeffer believes anyone can learn the skills necessary to become a powerful person, and he lays out a path toward improved social relationships.

Richard H. Thaler and Cass R. Sunstein, *Nudge: Improving Decisions about Health, Wealth, and Happiness*, revised and expanded edition (Penguin, 2009)

Thaler is a professor of economics at Cornell University and Sunstein is a professor of jurisprudence at the University of Chicago. In their book, the pair examine choices and how they are made. Illustrating their theories with academic research, Thaler and Sunstein explore why we make bad judgments and choices, and how we can improve our decision-making process. The book became a *New York Times* best seller and was a *Financial Times* best book of the year. The authors define a nudge as "anything that influences our choices" and explain how to move our lives in a better direction by changing how we interpret nudges and persuasive techniques.

Bibliography

David Allen, "When Office Technology Overwhelms, Get Organized"
New York Times, March 17, 2012
http://www.nytimes.com/2012/03/18/business/when-office-technology-overwhelms-get-organized.html?pagewanted=all&_r=1&

Amazon.com, "*Getting Things Done: The ABCs of Time Management*"
accessed May 21, 2013
http://www.amazon.com/Getting-Things-Done-ABCs-Management/dp/0684191970

Leo Babauta, "The Dirty Little Secrets of Productivity Bloggers"
Zenhabits (blog), August 24, 2008
http://zenhabits.net/the-dirty-little-secrets-of-productivity-bloggers/

Jeremy Caplan, "The Oracle of Organization"
Time, March 3, 2007
http://www.time.com/time/magazine/article/0,9171,1595223,00.html

Erin Doland, "GTD: A Revolutionary Idea in 1888"
Unclutterer (blog), September 11, 2008
http://unclutterer.com/2008/09/11/gtd-a-revolutionary-idea-in-1888/

James Fallows, "Organize Your Life!"
Atlantic, July 1, 2004
http://www.theatlantic.com/magazine/archive/2004/07/organize-your-life/303455/

Luc Glasbeek, "Edwin C. Bliss and 'Getting Things Done' "
Workplace Prosperity (blog), March 12, 2012
http://workplaceprosperity.com/2012/03/12/edwin-c-bliss-and-getting-things-done/

Ben Hammersley, "Meet the Man Who Can Bring Order to Your Universe"
Guardian, September 28, 2005
http://www.guardian.co.uk/technology/2005/sep/29/businesssense.businesssense

Keith H. Hammonds, "You Can Do Anything—But Not Everything"
Fast Company, April 30, 2000
http://www.fastcompany.com/40384/you-can-do-anything-not-everything

Francis Heylighen and Clément Vidal, "Getting Things Done: The Science behind Stress-Free Productivity"
Long Range Planning: International Journal of Strategic Management 41:6 (December 2008)
http://pespmc1.vub.ac.be/Papers/GTD-cognition.pdf

Paul Keegan, "How David Allen Mastered Getting Things Done"
Business 2.0: CNN Money, June 21, 2007
http://money.cnn.com/magazines/business2/business2_archive/2007/07/01/100117066/index.htm

J. Lebar, "Great Ideas in a Terrible Package," review of *Getting Things Done: The Art of Stress-Free Productivity*, by David Allen
Amazon.com, June 5, 2006
http://www.amazon.com/Getting-Things-Done-Stress-Free-Productivity/dp/0142000280

Lincoln Mullen, "Getting Back to Getting Things Done"
ProfHacker (blog), February 1, 2013
http://chronicle.com/blogs/profhacker/getting-back-to-getting-things-done/45741

Jane Porter, "7 Ways You're Wasting Time and Don't Even Know It"
Entrepreneur, July 31, 2012
http://www.entrepreneur.com/article/224090

Chris Taylor, "Getting Things Done Guru Goes Digital"
Fortune Small Business: CNN Money, July 20, 2009
http://money.cnn.com/2009/07/16/smallbusiness/getting_things_done_goes_digital.fsb/index.htm

James Temple, "David Allen on Staying on Track Amid Distractions"
San Francisco Chronicle, April 22, 2012
http://www.sfgate.com/business/article/David-Allen-on-staying-on-track-amid-distractions-3500082.php#ixzz2T7k70Hhx

Mary Whaley, review of *Getting Things Done: The Art of Stress-Free Productivity*, by David Allen
Booklist, December 15, 2000
http://www.amazon.com/Getting-Things-Done-Stress-Free-Productivity/dp/0670899240/ref=tmm_hrd_title_0

Gary Wolf, "*Getting Things Done* Guru David Allen and His Cult of Hyperefficiency"
Wired, September 25, 2007
http://www.wired.com/techbiz/people/magazine/15-10/ff_allen?currentPage=all

CPSIA information can be obtained at www.ICGtesting.com
Printed in the USA
BVOW07s1723221013

334362BV00001B/28/P

9 781623 151850